A New Awareness
INNER VISIONS SERIES #8

A New Awareness

by Jack Nast

First Edition published by
Life Enrichment Publications
Under ISBN 0-936275-00-6

International Standard Book Number 0-917086-94-5

Cover Design by Maria Kay Simms

Printed in the United States of America

Published by ACS Publications, Inc.
P.O. Box 16430
San Diego, CA 92116-0430

Dedication

This book is dedicated to my wife, Lori, who has taught me the meaning of unconditional love by giving me total freedom and support in pursuing this project. A unique individual who loves just about everyone, she has shown me how to look for the good in the world and has demonstrated the value of a positive approach to life. At first I mistook her childlike faith and imagination as naivete, but have since come to understand that it is really the most powerful directive force in the universe. In the intellectual world, answers can only be found when the proper logical procedures are followed, but in the world of intuition, answers come simply because you want them. In Lori's world, all things are possible because there is no doubt she can never see anything to limit options.

Contents

Foreword

I have written this simple allegory to convey a few basic truths to those who have been searching for a foundation in their universe. If we scrutinize every detail, life can seem extremely complex; but when we understand the whole in general, we find a wonderful simplicity that is relatively easy to comprehend. Nothing in the universe happens by chance. There is always a plan, and the outcome of each plan is improvement over what previously existed.

Humankind is now on the threshold of a major evolutionary shift in mental awareness. Circumstances and systems have aligned themselves in such a way that we must indeed wonder if we are seeing the "hand of God" at work. While the evolution of individuals seems to progress bit by bit, the evolution of humankind seems to progress from periods of stagnation into periodic quantum leaps. Historically we advanced from the pioneer stage into the industrial revolution, then into the atomic age and then the space age. Scientific achievement in the last century has grown out of all proportion with social, moral and religious understanding. Apparently the time has come for us to catch up.

I don't think anyone can give a rational explanation for it, but suddenly a new awareness is springing up in the minds of people throughout the world. It has been spontaneous. No one can take credit for organizing it, and few who have awakened to this new way of thinking understand where it came from.

Certainly spiritual and philosophic truths have been available for thousands of years, but only a few in each generation have reached out to embody them. They were the mystics, the thinkers, the messengers that served as a living memory for all humankind. But now millions are accepting it and have become hungry to learn more. Hundreds of pathways have been uncovered, and thousands of books have been written about all of the new clues to the old truths. At last, science, philosophy, sociology and religion are beginning to detect similarities which are pointing the way to convergent beliefs. Competition has turned into cooperation and, as a result, humankind is being viewed from an altogether different aspect. Humanity is now ready to plumb the depths of human potential.

Without a doubt we are entering the most exciting era in the known history of the human species. If we can learn to mobilize our common sense and psychic powers in time to avoid Armageddon, we will have an opportunity to emerge as masters of our own universe. Dualistic beliefs have been retarding our progress both as individuals and as a race. We must learn to serve one master — Positive Creativity. Nothing good has ever come from negative thought, so let us finally get rid of this anchor which has given us nothing but guilt, fear, pain, war and sickness.

Let us finally live in a world where God is not competing with the Devil and we are not competing with each other. The universe is infinitely abundant. Let us enjoy its fruits in peace and harmony and love. After all, we are all One.

CHAPTER ONE
THE MEETING

It was such a glorious morning that I could hardly remain seated at my desk. I tried to write but the ink dried on the tip of my quill before an idea could find expression on paper. My wandering gaze kept lifting my consciousness from desk top to the window which framed a lofty ridge of rugged mountains rising in all their splendor just to the east of my little cabin. The more I looked at the play of sunlight on the peaks, the more dingy and dull the interior of my cabin became. It seemed the mountain was calling me and, like a robot, I felt compelled to go.

Leaving everything on my desk, I wandered trancelike to the kitchen and began preparing sandwiches and drinks for my daypack. As I puttered about, I began to feel a slight tinge of inner urgency. It puzzled me. True, I was anxious to be on my way, but there was certainly no need for urgency.

As I bounded through the doorway, I felt like a schoolboy about to play hooky. Then my conscience grabbed at me and required me to go back to my desk for a pad and pencil so I would be prepared to write if the urge struck while wandering in the solitude of the hills.

The cool mountain air tasted sweet to my palate and a surge of energy rushed through my body as my lungs filled with their first breath of Mother Nature's vital elixir. I suddenly felt good all over and my tread was sure and light as I set my course for Lookout Rock at the very peak of Spirit Mountain.

The trail was smooth and well beaten as it meandered through the forests and foothills, but it became more rugged and difficult when it began to ascend the actual face of the mountain. It took several hours to negotiate the boulder-strewn path and I was exhausted when I reached the peak. After a brief rest, I searched for the trail markers that would lead me to Lookout Rock where the view of the valley below was said to be "awe inspiring." Now the sense of urgency within me had turned to anxiety and I found myself hurrying along the narrow path as though there were some sort of emergency.

I was practically breathless when I rounded the last outcropping of rock that hid my view of the valley floor. But before I could gather in the panoramic vista before me, I saw something that made my blood run cold. There, in a smooth hollow worn in the granite, lay the body of an old man. His still form was withered and ancient. I wondered how long he had been lying there. I approached cautiously. Dare I touch him?

"So you have finally come!" the body said in a surprisingly strong voice.

I snatched my hand from the leather-clad shoulder and fell over backwards, heart leaping from my chest. "My god, you're alive."

"It gladdens my heart to see that you are so observant. That is a good start," he said through a snaggle-toothed smile. "Since you seem bright eyed and alert now, perhaps we should get right into our mission. I have much to give you."

I stared into the weathered visage for a long moment. He was beardless but he had wrinkles on top of his wrinkles and his hair was the purest white I had ever seen. His dark eyes were powerful, piercing, but not intimidating. His features led me to believe he was an Indian but I could not begin to guess his tribe or his age.

"Am I supposed to know you?"

"No."

"Who are you? What are you doing up here?" I demanded.

"All in good time, my son. Please take out your pad and pencil so you may record all I have to say to you."

"How did you know I had a pad with me?" I asked astonishedly.

"Because I reminded you to get it from your desk before you set forth on your journey up the mountain." He smiled a knowing smile.

"What is this? Are you some sort of witch doctor?" I asked backing up a few paces.

"It depends on how you look at it. To some people I am a medicine man; to others a wizard, a prophet, messiah, a Christ or a Buddha. What difference does it make? What is in a name? Humanity is entering a whole new era of being and I have been sent to give illumination to them who sit in darkness and in the shadow of death. Through you I will guide their feet into the way of truth and peace."

"Wait a minute. What do you mean through me? I'm no religious leader or philosopher. I'm just a hack news reporter who has dreams of writing a book someday."

"That day has come. I give you this book as Moses was given a book, as Muhammad was given a book, as all who have spoken of wisdom have been given books. For as John prophesied in the Bible, 'When the spirit of truth has come, he will guide you in all truth; for he shall not speak of himself; but whatsoever he shall hear from God, that shall he speak; and he will show you things to come.' I am that nameless spirit of truth with no past and no future."

I thought to myself, "This must be a dream."

"It is no dream I assure you. You have been chosen to bring good tidings to the meek — to bind up the brokenhearted, to proclaim liberty to the captives and to open the prison for those who are bound in fear. The spirit of God has rested upon you and you will be given the spirit of wisdom and understanding."

"How did you know what I was thinking?"

"There is but one mind," he answered calmly.

"I don't get it. Exactly what are you trying to tell me?"

"The truth of who and what human beings really are and who and what they can become if enough souls agree to change."

"Well, look, I'm kind of a simple man and I'm not sure I will be able to understand it myself much less pass it on to other people," I protested uncomfortably. "You see, I'm not long on intellect. I kind of do things by the seat of my pants — you know, intuition, hunches. I think you should get someone who is smarter.''

"Moses, Buddha and Muhammad all said the same thing when they were called, so you are in good company. It is because of the power of your instinct that you were chosen. Intellect is a slave of the ego. Intuition is a direct channel to God. Sit and open your mind,'' he commanded.

I did as he asked because I couldn't think of anything else to do.

"Two thousand years ago Pontius Pilate asked Christ if he were a king. Jesus told him he was born and came into the world only to bear witness to the truth. He knew that everyone searching for the truth would hear his words and understand. Truth is the pathway to personal evolution. Jesus also said 'that the comforter which is the Holy Ghost, whom your father has sent, shall teach you all things, and bring all things to your remembrance, whatsoever I have said to you, for the Holy Ghost shall teach you in the same hour what you ought to know. You will know *from within* that I speak the truth.' ''

"I don't like to appear ignorant, but what is that supposed to mean?''

"In other words, the real you already knows the truth, while the physical you denies it. The truth is always revealed to you as your time comes to receive it. If all the wisdom in the universe were dumped over all the people of the world, they would each absorb only what they were capable of understanding at that particular time.''

"What do you mean when you refer to the real me?''

"Every religion has taught it over and over again. You are spirit. It is the spirit that grows. The flesh profiteth nothing. This is the first truth you must absorb. All the lessons learned on Earth are for the evolution of the immortal spirit. When your physical body has outlived its usefulness, it will be cast aside.

"Now, to continue, many religions have brought truth to people, but Christianity contributed a little something extra because it encouraged individual and collective liberty, a belief in self, democracy, education and real freedom. It was first expressed in terms needed for understanding two thousand years ago just as I will retell the truth now in the terms of your times. It is the same truth, whether you call it the brotherhood of humanity made one in a fatherhood of God, or the individual degrees of consciousness operating in evolution toward the perfection of the whole of Consciousness. I must impress on you at this time that Consciousness is the **only reality**,'' he stated positively.

"It has been decided that the people of the world need a new presentation of the truth in light of their own time and in terms of their own knowledge so that all may seek truth's comfort for themselves and find it if they will.

"So one of the first things needed most by the human race at this time is a renewal of faith in its own immortality. Worldwide acceptance of immortality will bring back stability and comfort to mankind. In fact, only by a reestablishment of the old faith in the continuity, worthwhileness, the purpose and responsibility of life, can people or nations regain that stability.

"Stability is what you have lost and are now seeking to regain. Not security. Security is material. Stability is spiritual. Stability is the soul, the character of peoples. Given that, the individual or nation makes its own security. But real foundation rock, unwavering stability, no person can have without faith in immortality. For without immortality, Earth life would have no point.

"If life on Earth is all, why bother with it? Why bring children into the world? Why plan ahead for future generations? You must know that the I Am of humanity is in evolution, and must go on whether you know it or not. Human beings have become so engrossed in the wonders of their own obstructed universe that they have allowed themselves to become confused and overawed by things outside themselves. The world is in mourning now because it has lost much that it once valued, emotionally and materially. It will find comfort only in truth."

"Why has this been allowed to happen? Why haven't we been given the truth?" I asked.

"You have been given the truth many times. Holy books are full of clues to the truth, but unfortunately they have become hidden amongst false ideas and church symbology. It has become my duty to restate them, or perhaps reinterpret them in modern terms. If you search, you will find many clues to a clearer understanding of your role in the universe. All people are one with God, and God is all there is. How you assimilate this truth is your own business since your greatest gift is free will. You are free to express life any way you wish, moving through spiritual evolution at your own pace. You will always evolve in spite of yourself but it need not be so frustrating. The human race has come to a point in evolution where consciousness must be plowed and, with your help, I will do just that.''

"You must be kidding. Do you honestly believe that by telling me all of these things on top of a mountain, you are going to change the world? Nobody down there will believe me and I doubt if anyone even cares."

"Take my word for it, very little happens on Earth without a plan. Each new day is a scene in a play and each of the actors write their own script. Everything is in evolution, and although growth is on an individual basis, there are different eras of humankind, and humanity is on the threshold of a new era, a new age, a new awareness."

"How do you know? I haven't seen any evidence of it. It looks to me as though people are still engaged in war, still killing each other, still stealing, cheating and robbing. So what's new?" I asked.

"You are the typical pessimistic news reporter, always looking for the ugly side of life. Look about you. Can't you see, can't you feel a different attitude growing in the hearts of men and women throughout the world? Can't you sense it? In spite of the acts of terrorism or perhaps because of them, people are joining together in love. As a group, they are more concerned and giving. They are more hopeful, more positive about the future and more thoughtful of their fellow humans. Little by little those who beat the drums of Armageddon are fading into the background while leaders of vision and promise gain the forefront.

"After thousands of years of war and four decades under the threat of atomic annihilation, humankind is ready to evolve into a new order of being. The human race has finally been frightened enough to fight back. It is finally desperate enough to reach out for a new truth, a new sense of reality. The masses, the flock, the public, the majority, have allowed themselves to be pushed, badgered and terrorized by crazy idealists, governments, religions, science and the news media. This has been so because people have not been willing to accept responsibility for themselves. Each was born a free spirit, and from the moment of birth, they have relinquished that freedom bit by bit until they were totally under the control of other human beings to whom they had given their power. Little by little they destroyed their faith in their own ability and placed faith in everything and everybody but God.

"Because they have always been so lazy about guarding personal freedom, people have looked to some form of government to take care of them. More often than not, the government became the problem rather than the solution. The lives of billions of souls down through the ages have been completely influenced by the quality of leadership they have chosen. Sometimes it was good and sometimes horrible. But whatever it was, it came about with the permission of the majority. No, let me rephrase that, it came about at the insistence of the majority. You see, the power of the mass mind is awesome. We must make people aware of it as soon as possible. This is very important. Every major happening in the world scene is a result of mass belief. Everything from clothing trends to stock market fluctuations, from music to catastrophe, from philosophic truth to Armageddon, everything has been created by the power of mass belief. The Earth plane of existence is a manifestation of mass soul energy. Every change is caused by a shift in the energy."

"If that is true, why would people allow anything to go wrong? Why would they put their energy into war and misery?"

"As I have said, there is always a plan. The stage is always set for the greater lesson. For millenia the majority focused on the negative use of this power, primarily because of fear. Some who understood universal laws took advantage of this fear and learned to control others through it. These individuals cannot be blamed since the majority allowed them to do it by relinquishing individual power to their leader. Since all people are born with equal power, there is no way one individual can rule another unless allowed. An individual who understands the true nature of inner being can never become a slave to another. The time has come to know who you are."

"There have been many examples of leadership on both sides of the coin and all have served a purpose. For instance, did you ever wonder how a paperhanger from Austria became the ruler of Germany? You know it certainly wasn't because of his physical prowess. Hitler was a small, unimposing man, but he recognized the power of an idea and, like a magnet, he attracted support for his dream. He made his goal the goal of a nation and it became so because millions supported him. The more his power grew, the more others feared it, and that fear contributed to his growing authority. You see, when you fear something, it means you believe it can happen. It is faith in the negative. If you don't want to bring something bad into your life, don't fear it. Destroy it by turning the fear into something positive and constructive."

"You should have told that to the Jews before Hitler got a foothold," I said.

"The story of the Jews under Hitler was a lesson within a lesson. All of the players were simply acting out the prophecy of the Jewish national belief in suffering. It was prophesied, and generations of Jews saw to it that they were scattered from their lands, abused by everyone and finally led back to the promised land. Even though they were citizens of many countries, they always maintained a consciousness of Israeli nationalism. Of course, this attitude of separateness always led to problems. They created prejudice by their own feelings of differentness. They were never just another religious group to be absorbed by the culture of a country. They were always a separate nation within a nation. They took the ancient prophecies as their script and proceeded to act it out for thousands of years. A perfect example of the power of mass belief."

"If what you say is true, the world could be in big trouble. With a belief in nuclear war, world hunger, chemical poisoning, air pollution, water pollution and overpopulation on everybody's mind, it's almost inevitable that the world will be destroyed like it says in the Bible."

"Ah! Now you have hit on the crux of the matter. This is why I am here. You see, it is a belief in the end of the world that is the underlying factor in all of this. It is the fundamental misinterpretation of the Book of Revelation along with a blatant misunderstanding of Christ's message that is at the core. First it was the Jews and now it is the Christians who want to behave like lemmings who must run to the sea of self-destruction. The Jews caused their own misery and suffered it as a people, but some Christians believe they alone will be saved by Christ while the rest of the world is destroyed. Our job is to change enough minds so it won't happen.''

CHAPTER TWO
GOD AND HUMANS

I stared at the wrinkled old man for a long moment trying to comprehend what he was telling me. The wind swept the clouds from the face of the sun and the warmth was reassuring.

"You know, old man, you're really beginning to scare me. Are you trying to tell me that my job is to save the world?"

"Yes," he replied simply.

"Are you going to tell me how, or am I just supposed to know?"

"The plan is simple. There are roughly five billion souls on Earth now and many of them believe in the end-of-the-world concept. You will have to either change enough minds or raise enough consciousness against the idea to neutralize it. As soon as you muster a critical counterforce, the old idea will dissolve and the new idea will take its place. You are all linked to one creative mind."

"How am I going to convince anybody? I don't know anything about religion or philosophy," I pleaded.

"Wrong. You know everything about it."

"No. I'm telling you, you have the wrong guy. I swear I don't know anything."

"There is but one mind and you are tapped into it. You automatically recognize the truth as it is revealed to you."

"Well maybe nobody has ever revealed it to me."

"Ask what you need and I will explain," he answered confidently.

"Do you know everything?"

"Yes. Ask."

I figured I might as well clear up the big one first. "OK, who or what is God?"

"God is all there is: time, space, motion, matter, the all-creating consciousness; a fluidic, ever-changing, ever-growing creative force. It is everywhere in the universe and there is only One Universe. All that is is contained within it. We are all immersed in an infinite intelligence we call God, and its most powerful aspect is Love."

"I'd like to know how everything began. Is the Bible version, or should I say versions, correct?"

"First you must understand that there really is no beginning or end. But since people cannot comprehend infinity, I will try to phrase what is in terms you can understand at your level," the Indian explained patiently.

"In the beginning there was only spirit or intelligence. There was no visible form, nothing but the life principle. Then God awakened and began to create. Desiring to manifest in form, this great consciousness did so through the power of his word. God is pure intelligence and endless being. His basic nature is to create. However, since he was all, he had to act within himself. Understand here that I use the masculine gender only because God is most commonly recognized as a father figure in your terms. God has no gender in reality. It is the Father/Mother of everything. Everything that is is contained within God: the word, which is the mold; the energy; and the substance to fill the mold. All manifestations have substance.

"Recently your scientists have discovered what they call the 'superforce' or that power which encompasses all. They now know that space, time, matter and everything else can be generated from nothingness. They also know that within the superforce is contained four basic forces: gravity, electromagnetic force, and two nuclear forces simply called strong and weak. All four are vital to your present existence.

"It has been known for some time that all of the interactions in the universe can be shown to be the consequence of these four. Gravity holds you to the Earth and the Earth to the sun.

The electromagnetic force holds atoms and molecules together; manifested as light, it enables you to see. The strong force holds the atomic nucleus together, enabling complex atoms to exist. The weak force controls the reactions on the atomic level that allow the sun to shine.

"Science has also discovered the fundamental building blocks or particles which are acted upon by these forces. They have called them quarks for some unexplainable reason. In any event, they know these particles are indivisible, with no spatial dimensions; yet they have properties like mass, electric charge and spin. Although it has not yet been discovered, everything and anything in the universe can be made manifest through the use of quarks. Now, you know, imagination is the mold, superforce is the energy and quarks are the substance that fill the mold. This is how God and human beings create.

"I didn't mean to get sidetracked but I wanted to point out how close science is coming to discovering God in its own way. Physics and quantum mechanics are beginning to uncover what has been known philosophically for thousands of years. Since modern society is impressed by scientific discoveries, it will open itself to the truth more easily. This will help you."

"Where does humanity come into this picture?" I asked.

"Actually, humanity as you know it is a creation of the soul. Each human being is a soul entity or just one dimension of the soul. But to make it more understandable at this point, let me say that when God finished creating the mechanical universe, he was not satisfied. He decided to create a being that had real life within itself. In order to accomplish this, he had to implant his own creative nature in this being and make it in his own image and likeness. This was the soul created out of the stuff of eternity. You see, in order to have real life, the soul had to partake of the true nature of divinity. So God created it from the essence of himself and gave it free will or self choice.

"As a soul entity, humans were not automatic; instead they were spontaneous and were given dominion over everything of lesser intelligence. They were given the privilege of naming everything God created as it unfolded and was recognized by him. And so it was that God gave people dominion over all earthly things to enjoy in the fullness and completeness of his own nature,'' he explained.

"In other words, the soul entity you call human is spirit organized by consciousness. A part of God which is in evolution. The physical person you see before you is merely a manifestation of the spirit, constructed to experience life on the Earth plane through the five senses. The physical you is a creation of the spiritual you.''

"Why did we create a physical self or this plane of existence? How did it come about?'' I asked.

"The Earth is a theater for experience and evolution. At first the spirit of humanity roamed free across the face of this planet. Like children, various souls entered the material world in different aspects, tasting and testing the infinite combinations the Earth offered through the five senses. In order to experience all that the Father/Mother had given them, the souls projected themselves into a variety of living things. They not only wanted to observe but to sense life on the physical plane. As time went on, they began to inhabit animal forms more than any other since this mold seemed to offer the most diversity of experience. Some of these animal forms were similar in looks to what you call human today. However, in those days, the human animal took many shapes and sizes from that of a pygmy to those of giants. In their experimenting, they sometimes mixed the human form with those of animals as was depicted in your mythology.

"Eventually, the ideal form was developed. Let us call it the Adam prototype. This form, which is quite similar to those found on Earth today, was projected into five locations as the five races with five physical senses.''

"What about women? Where did they come into the picture?''

"At first the spirit of humanity was androgynous, containing both sexes within itself, but later it split and became man and woman as in the Adam and Eve allegory. This was necessary because polarity or sex was one of the key principles of the universe. The division of the genders, not so apparent on other planes, was a fascinating discovery.''

"How long did people live then?''

"During that early period, souls remained in the physical body six hundred to a thousand years and more. It was because of this long duration that they began to lose contact with the spiritual side of their nature. In a way, they became entrapped in the cloak of materialism they had donned for their own diversion. Eventually they began to misuse their creative powers in self-indulgence and became subject to the Law of Cause and Effect. This then established the Earth as a theater for a new kind of expression. It became the first stage in the individualization of the soul."

CHAPTER THREE
THE BEGINNING

I didn't know what to think about what the man was telling me but he had certainly aroused my curiosity. Questions whirled in my head like numbers in a bingo basket. I had to know more.

"What was the purpose of all this?"

"You see, Earth is a kind of borning place. It is one of the first learning experiences for a young soul. The physical body is contained within the soul and is an instrument whereby the soul gains evolutionary growth through the process of many lives and life experiences."

"I want to make sure I understand this very clearly," I stated deliberately. "You are saying that we absolutely never die?"

"The physical body of necessity experiences what you call death, but the soul, or real self, is immortal and eternal since it is one with God."

"Well, OK then, if Earth is the borning place, when and where did all this stuff begin?"

"The human race has been on Earth much longer than you suspect. The actual amount of sidereal time has little meaning in the universe, but in your terms, more than ten million years. The world as such, has no beginning and no end but there have been definite eras of humankind. Many civilizations, several much more highly developed in the sciences than the current one, have come and gone."

"Why haven't we found more evidence of them?"

"In many cases you have, but did not recognize it as

evidence. For instance, what if your people had found a microchip just fifty years ago? Would they have known what it was? A civilization must attain a level equal to or above the one it is examining before the scientific achievements can be appreciated. However, a more significant reason for not finding more evidence is that the planet's surface has been re-plowed for new plantings many times. Mountains have grown and collapsed. Seas have moved over different areas. The poles have shifted more than once. Areas now cold were once hot and tropical. Great fertile areas are now desert, and the farmland of today was once beneath the sea.''

"Where was the Garden of Eden?"

He laughed and shook his head. "That which became known as the Garden of Eden was on the continent of Atlantis which originally stretched from what is now the Gulf of Mexico to the doors of the Mediterranean. Because you are living in a relatively static period, you have come to believe the Earth's surface was formed through slow evolvement but this is not so. During the last period of cataclysms, at least three great civilizations sank beneath the sea where their remains still lie. This condition was a result of humanity's belief system at the time and was the basis of the end-of-the-world stories carried forward to this day and time. Somehow, history became prophecy.''

CHAPTER FOUR

REINCARNATION

"If I may, I'd like to backtrack for a moment," I said. "When you answered an earlier question, you said the soul was in evolutionary growth and gained experience through many lives. Were you talking about reincarnation?"

"As I have said, the spirit is immortal and in evolution. There are many possible combinations of experience on the Earth plane, therefore we have a system which you call reincarnation."

"How does it work?"

"The physical world is created by all who live within it at one time. Every individual becomes manifest by an arrestment of frequency or a slowing down from spirit to material. Later, when the physical body is discarded, the soul-stuff or spirit of the individual merely changes frequency and moves to an intermediate level still attached to the Earth but much less obstructed. This soul may still sense Earth life and in many ways more vividly than when embodied in human form. For now, unencumbered by the human body, it is more aware of the true nature of itself and the universe around it. Each soul is uniquely individual and endowed by the Creator with free will. It may experience any phase of life, any condition and any emotion it wishes. It may grow and learn at whatever pace it chooses. All are learning, all are growing, but each is working toward truth on different paths.

"While in the unobstructed or spiritual state, many souls get together and plan the next set of Earth circumstances that will serve them best for future evolution. Every problem, every relationship, each environment and even parents are chosen at this time. This is really the stage during which true free will is exercised. At this level you know who you are, what you are doing and what you hope to accomplish. This then is where the blueprint for your next life or Earth experience is laid out."

"We create ourselves?"

"The oversoul is your creator and it endows your Earthly soul entity with the same powers of free will that it has. But that free will operates within the restricted bonds of the five senses, emotion and ego. You can overcome these factors but only as you recognize them. For in the Earth existence, you are shut off from the real you. Sometimes it takes hundreds of lifetimes to gain the desired level. After many Earth experiences, a soul reaches a certain plateau of illumination and moves to the next level of spiritual existence," the wise man explained.

"But who determines these things?"

"There are a number of immutable laws which keep all things in balance. People have free will and certain powers but they cannot change the Law. God is all, he is the Creator. Humanity never really creates; all people are able to imagine has already been created. Individuals simply reveal the truth as it unfolds for them at their individual level of understanding."

"I don't think I'm quite clear on what you're saying."

"I will give you an example," he answered patiently. "If you can imagine each life as a play with all of the actors involved in its creation — with all of the actors having a personal stake — with all of the actors playing a role for their personal growth, while understanding that the growth of all is imperative to the evolution of the whole, then you have the basic concept of the Earth experience in the scheme of things.

"Because of the interdependence of all of the actors, you must realize all the more that you are your brother's keeper. You are all a part of the same Consciousness as individual drops of water are a part of the ocean."

"But what's the point in creating this gigantic illusion?"

"In each life, the individual puts on different bodies as you would costumes. People may be rich in one life, poor in another;

healthy in one, sickly in another; male or female, black, white, yellow, brown or red; they could be born to any nation or any parents.''

''You mean all of us get to experience even the different races?''

''Yes. Every racial group has its virtues and its faults, each one offering a special kind of opportunity physically and spiritually for development. The same is true for nations and churches. Each meets a psychological and spiritual need of its members. Each must be respected. Each must be seen as a piece of the puzzle that will one day become the perfect self. God is all things to all people. The system has been established so that all may know him. There is not one group better than another.''

''Why is all of this necessary?''

''All learning comes through experience. It is the key to the adventure of living. When the individual has experienced all, it will recognize no form of prejudice for it will have been all before it is done. The choice in each life is governed by the **Law of Cause and Effect** or **Karma**. The Law, however, is modulated by the individual through what you call conscience. **Nothing that happens to a person is as important as what he or she thinks of it**,'' he emphasized. ''For each is his own judge.

''Is Earth life predestined then?''

''No. Karma is not fate, but cause and effect. It can govern you when you don't understand it but it can also serve you when you understand the truth about it.''

CHAPTER FIVE

THOUGHT

"How much creative power do we have and how do we use it?"

"People are created in the image of God in that they are part of the whole and have certain cocreative powers within the limits of their frequencies on the Earth plane. Each human is constantly creating his or her own individual experience and has the power of choice at all times. Everything, I repeat, everything, a person thinks is projected out into the universe. I cannot stress this enough. Thoughts are things. The more vividly a thought is imagined, the more power is given to it. In this way, people create their own environment, friends, enemies, lifestyle, fortunes or lack thereof. Negative thinking is just as powerful as positive thinking since the Law is set up to provide anything a person wants without distinction. It is impartial."

"Are you trying to tell me that we get everything we think?" I asked in amazement. "You mean even the bad stuff as well as the good?"

"Exactly. Thought is the creative power. You are both the benefactor and the victim of your own thinking. When you awake each morning, you have at least two choices. You can be happy or you can be sad. If you choose happiness, your experience will be good all day. On the other hand, if you allow worries or fears to dominate your thinking, you will get unhappy results. All negative thinking is error or, as you call it, sin. This is your real enemy, not the Devil. Satan is merely a creation of human imagination. It gives people someone outside of themselves to blame for all of their own negative creations. The only wall between physical humans and spiritual reality is the ego. The object of Earth life is to evolve beyond the ego. The original allegory about Satan was really meant to demonstrate how the human ego turned from the will of God. Symbolically, the Devil is humanity's will or ego. The fallen angel.''

"If what you say is true, then thought properly directed could be a very powerful tool," I said thoughtfully.

"That is true. It is far and away the greatest power in the universe with the exception of God itself. The power of thought, in the hands of those who know how to direct it, is infinite. Everything you could possibly imagine is there for the asking. All you have to do is know how to ask. God does not judge and is not selective. Ask and ye shall receive. But, ye shall receive only in the amount ye believe ye should receive. That is the only limit. But don't forget, this holds true for all of your negative creations as well.

"There are many who have gotten what they wanted on this Earth and did so with no knowledge of the Law. They didn't know it existed but they knew how to ask. They imagined what they wanted and believed it was their divine right to have it. Then they went out and got it.

"Although God is not electricity, your use of it is analogous to thought demands on the God power. Few people understand the theory of electricity but most people know how to use it. Let us suppose the electric company were God, making its energy available to all people without cost. By following the right procedures, anyone could tap into the power source for whatever individual use they may have: lights, heat, toaster, iron, hot water, oven or refrigerator. The person knows the power is there and if a switch is turned on, contact can be made between the appliance and the power source. It makes no difference how much electricity the appliance demands nor what appliance is attached; the source simply supplies it. And so it is with the Law. The power source for everything is God and it is limitless. If you have total faith and know that it works, it will not fail you. It cannot.

"The problem with humans is that their egos have convinced them they are the Creator, and therefore people have lost faith in any power beyond themselves. They want to take credit for all the positive creations and to blame someone else for all the negative ones. When ego enters the picture, people forget to screw the light bulb into the socket. Instead, they hold the bulb in their hands and try to will it to light. If it doesn't work, they figure the Devil must be stopping it or that it wasn't God's will. People must come to the understanding that the ego can create nothing, but if they can shove the ego aside, humanity has the ability to direct all of the power there is for whatever they want. The will is a necessary human quality on the physical plane, but the way to get things done is through faithful receptivity.

"The Law always works and is always giving what you ask whether you know it or not. There can be a boomerang effect to thought which is sometimes a side effect of judgment. If for instance you loan a friend money and later have doubts about his honesty or desire to repay you, he will sense it and lend thought energy to your negative idea. The result could be bitterness, animosity and nonpayment of the debt. You must understand that everyone is an intuitive mind reader at the subconscious level. Your minds are all connected into the one Universal Mind. People will become what you expect of them. If you see trust, they will be trustworthy."

"That's pretty scary. You make it sound like there is no such thing as private thought. Are we really linked up that closely?"

"Yes. As you understand more, you will learn how to use your individual energy without feeling separate from the whole. You are like a troop of scouts gathering wood for a bonfire. Each selects the stick that best expresses the self, but the end result is one fire for the benefit of all.

CHAPTER SIX

KARMA

"What about Karma and the laws of cause and effect?"

"It is in a much greater sense that the laws of Karma take effect. If a person develops lifelong prejudices and judgments, chances are the person will get an opportunity to experience exactly what has been judged. If you hate people because of the color of their skin, you will more than likely be born of that race in an ensuing life. The same is true of nationalities, religion or sex. The more you judge and despise in one life, the more likely you are to experience it in another. You must understand however, that this is not done in the form of punishment. It is simply the individual's need to understand that kind of experience in order to grow. It is not, as has been previously thought, a law of retribution. It is your own choice."

"Don't you think that being born crippled or retarded is punishment no matter where it comes from?"

"In your consciousness a person is likely to think it is retribution or punishment to be born crippled or impoverished, but in reality the individual is learning a valuable lesson. Such a life might be a greater opportunity for spiritual growth than being born healthy and wealthy. Remember, the choice was yours. You must understand, that anytime during the play you know you have learned the lesson, you may change your role. Usually you will know whether or not there is any value left in the experience. If however, you have not really solved your problem, it will continue to come into every experience you have no matter what role you choose to play.

"Karma is a law of obligatory balance. An individual who causes something to be out of balance is responsible for putting things back the way he or she found them. If the problem is recognized at once, the imbalance can be corrected by the soul. The longer it remains uncorrected, the greater the division within the soul and the more severe its entrapment in Earth systems.

"Karma is also a law which has been accepted for the programming of life dramas. When you know your true self, you will only accept those suggestions, ideas and hang-ups that suit your purpose at this time. You are always free and therefore not at the mercy of a neurosis from a past life, nor are there any fears from your present life that you cannot conquer. You may or may not conquer them according to your understanding. It is entirely up to you.

"You create the conditions within which you live as a challenge to yourself. You are free to use all the courage and resolution you can muster to solve the problems. You do not place them like lead weights around your neck hoping ahead of time that you will drown. You set these goals in hopes that you will solve them. Each lifetime begins with a plan and a potential pattern of instructive experience or creative fulfillment — not predestination, but a road map.

"With its free will, a soul may conform to the plan or deviate from it. The strategy of the soul requires constant adjustment to new conditions resulting from choices made. When the soul entity follows its guiding influence, the life plan will be fulfilled. Whenever there is little or no attunement to higher intelligence, the life pattern unfolds by trial and error. The personality has been given the greatest gift of all; you get exactly what you want to get. You create from nothing the experience that is your own. If you do not like your experience, then look within yourself and change it. But realize also that you are responsible for your joys and triumphs and that the energy to create any of these realities comes from the inner self. What you do with it is up to you. You are not programmed. Nothing happens because it must happen. Every thought that you have now changes reality. Not just yours, but all of reality."

"You mean there is no such thing as predestiny then?"

"Predestiny in the physical world was created by the real or spiritual you before you were born. If you come to the realization of who you really are, you can consciously change your fate."

"How can we change it?"

"There are a number of ways. If you feel the current life experience is unprofitable, you could change it by getting rid of the physical body, or, as you call it, dying. You could repair the condition through what you call miracles. Heal yourself physically, mentally, or financially by directing the power of God through faith. Results may not occur as dramatically as with a bolt of lighting or a puff of smoke, but I assure you these changes are occurring all over the world every day.

"The sick are healed, others change attitude and use their handicap for good purposes; many have fought their way out of poverty and squalor into great wealth; others rise from obscurity to fame. It is being done constantly. Whatever is possible for one is possible for all. Remember, the Law is not selective."

There hath no temptation taken you but such as is common to man: but God is faithful, who will not suffer you to be tempted above that ye are able; but will with the temptation also make a way to escape, that ye may be able to bear it.

I Corinthians 10:13

CHAPTER SEVEN

SOUL

"Tell me something about the soul."

"It is strange that most people believe they have a soul but they never ask what a soul is. They simply think of it as a spiritual object in their possession." He said thoughtfully. "I would like to clear up that point. The soul is not something you possess, it is what you are."

"But what about this salvation of the soul that we are all supposed to be working on?"

"I'm sorry you have been disillusioned but the soul is not something you must save or redeem after death. It is not bound by its present ventures in one life alone nor will it be judged accordingly after death on the basis of a few paltry years. The soul is the highest expression of life. It is the most highly motivated, most highly energized and most potent consciousness unit in the universe.

"The soul is free. It stands at the center of itself, exploring, extending its capacities in all directions at once. It is involved in many legitimate issues of creativity. It is never static. It is ever expanding, changing and evolving. It is in a constant state of becoming. The doors of the soul are always open and they lead to all dimensions of experience. It has no limits. The universal soul that is you experiences life both inside and outside the fabric of physical life as you know it. It is a multidimensional being capable of experiencing life in many aspects of the universe at one time.

"Each part of the soul contains the whole, and the experience of each part enriches all the other parts. It is an open-ended spiritual system. It is part of you as God is part of you and when you realize that it is God's energy that forms you and is an intimate part of you, you will no longer need to create separate gods who exist outside your universe. Nor will you have to perceive the soul as some distant entity."

"What happens to individual personalities after we die? Do we all return to God?"

"There is no reason for the ego to fear loss of its identity. For each individual maintains an identity in the Law through personal use of it. Each person is drawing from life what each thinks into it. There is, within, a mental law which is working out the will and purpose of your conscious thoughts. Your personality and individuality are part of your soul and are equally indestructible and immortal. They are constantly there, constantly aware, and perceive in a constant way but are in a state of change as each new experience enriches them. You are not fated to dissolve into All That Is. All aspects of your personality, as you presently understand them, will be retained. God is the creator of individuality, not the means of its destruction."

CHAPTER EIGHT
GOD AND RELIGION

"While we're on the subject of God and gods, how about shedding a little light on the relationship between God and our religions?"

"First I must tell you that all the mind, spirit and intelligence you can find within yourself is as much of the original, creative God as you can understand as an individual. When you are able to see yourself as you are, you will be able to perceive God as he is. Right now, you have no choice but to see by looking through your own eyes. Human beings will find a better God when they arrive at a higher standard for themselves. If God is to interpret himself to humans, he must do it through humans. This is where the prophets, sages and religious teachers come in."

"Are you trying to tell me that people create their own God?"

"Yes. Before the Hebrews conceived of a judgmental god, many ancient peoples believed in a more lenient deity. They knew that an inner spirit pervaded every living thing and they often addressed that spirit within animals, plants and birds, but they were also well aware of the overall spirit of which the lesser spirits were but a part. I must point out that their belief was a better representation of inner reality than the angry, overseer God invented by the Hebrews."

"But I thought the Hebrews were God's chosen people?"

"They were the chosen people of their God. For it was under the Hebrew concept of God that people became more aware of their egos. You see, early humans observed nature and let it reveal its secrets to them, but later, under the Hebrew god, humanity developed a sense of power over nature. That god became mankind's ally against nature.

"In reading the Old Testament, you must realize that the Hebrew concept of God was actually a symbol of unleashed human ego. His actions were those of a spoiled child with too much power. Whenever he was angered, he sent out thunder, lightning and fire to destroy his enemies. He was a god of punishment and reward. Under this concept, the emerging human ego brought forth emotional and psychological problems and challenges. Humanity's sense of separation from nature grew, and nature became a tool to use against others.

"During this period, the god inside people became the god outside, and human beings developed a new realm in which their awareness was projected outward into the physical world instead of being focused on inner reality."

"Are you saying all of people's problems began with the Jews? You mean it was their fault things got so screwed up?"

The old man smiled. "There are no Jews, Christians, Hindus or Muslims in eternity. You must understand that all of this was part of your freedom to create your own world. It was time to try new challenges, so humanity stepped out of a psychological existence into a physical world where people could study the process of their own consciousness. You see, in order to do this, individuals had to separate themselves from the inner spontaneity which had given them peace and security. They had to burn all of the bridges to inner reality so they could look outward and initiate an independent focus. Once this was accomplished, perception of the exterior universe changed and it became alien and apart from the one who perceived it. God then became an idea projected outward, independent of the individual and divorced from nature. He became a reflection of the emerging human ego with all its brilliance, savagery, power and intent for mastery. From that time forward, the characteristics of God changed as human egos changed. The various perceptions of gods have simply been the perceptions of mankind's own consciousness projected outward. Each individual has his or her own unique perception of God."

"Do you mean to infer now that there is no real God except the one we imagine?"

"No. You must understand always that behind each drama, each experiment, each development, is one Universal Intelligence. The one reality. Humanity's perception of it cannot change the Changeless."

CHAPTER NINE

EGO

"You have discussed God in terms of the human ego, but what is your concept of the ego?"

"The ego is a result of the propulsion of inner characteristics outward into a focus on the physical world. Without a doubt, its development has had immeasurable consequences on inner reality at the subjective level. Since the ego was born from within, it has always struggled for independence while carrying a nagging certainty of its inner origin. Once established, the ego feared for its position, afraid that it would dissolve back into the inner self from which it sprang."

"So is the ego good or bad then?"

"Because of the difficulties mankind has seemingly suffered since the development of the ego, it might appear to have been a terrible turn of events for the soul of humanity. However, the emergence of ego provided the inner self with a new kind of feedback. It not only gave a different view of itself, but allowed the inner self a chance to see possibilities for development of which it had not been previously aware. You must always remember that the inner self is in a constant state of growth."

"Why do people fear death?"

"When human beings were still in communication with nature, death was not feared as it is in your civilization today, for the cycle of consciousness was understood. In considering immortality, people seem to hope for further egotistical development and yet object to the idea that such development might involve change.

"You see, personality is in a state of constant change and quite often does so in unpredictable ways. Because of their egos, human beings try desperately to cling to certain patterns they perceive as unique to them. In doing this, they are prevented from seeing the self as it really is. The ego has opened some interesting channels of experience, but it is a very small part of the multidimensional soul.

"As long as humans identify themselves with the ego, the fear of death will always have a hold on them. Once people have freed themselves of the ego and understand that the center of consciousness is in the immortal self, death will become an adventure. When you die, you will be free of this illusion and the obstructed universe you now live in. You will return to the absolute truth and become united with God.

"Those who identify themselves with ego undergo confused and sometimes suffering transformations. But those who glimpse the greater self take death calmly. Assured of immortality and stability of spirit, they pass from one world to another easily. Their spirits simply lay down their bodies because they are finished with them."

CHAPTER TEN

REALITY

"After all of the things you have told me, I'm not sure I understand what reality is anymore. Could you clear this up for me?" I asked.

"Reality includes every condition and circumstance possible in the universe. Nothing exists outside its scope. Every condition is governed by a perfect system of laws, and every circumstance is the result of cause and effect," the old sage explained automatically.

"Why are you revealing all of this now in such scientific terms?"

"Because, as I have stated, mankind has finally arrived at the age of the individual where an entity's search for reality is primarily for his or her own enlightenment. Worldwide education has reached a high-enough level that most should be able to grasp the truth of reality once they let go of old concepts. The ideal situation will arrive when the individual masters his or her life pattern and brings it into alignment with reality. Therefore, research into the nature of reality should be the business of any thinking person who recognizes that destiny is individual, not collective. Although we are all connected in one mind, evolution is not a group project."

"Where do good and evil come into this picture?"

"You create your own reality and live in it according to your inner beliefs, therefore you should be very careful of the beliefs you choose to accept. You see, good and evil exist in each person's mind as they choose to believe. In reality, there are no devils or demons. Good and evil effects are basically illusions, but they do have a certain validity in your present system of reality. Since they are a part of your root assumptions, you must learn how to deal with them.''

"What purpose do good and evil serve in the whole scheme of things?''

"It is a bit difficult to explain since in your present state of consciousness you do not perceive the whole picture. You cannot yet understand the deep unities that opposites represent. The seemingly disruptive effects of opposites actually stem from your lack of perception. You are viewing a multifaceted concept from a one-dimensional aspect. Since you must operate within the world as you perceive it, then opposites will appear to be conditions of existence. You must learn about all aspects of anything before you can understand the whole.

"If you lived on one side of a coin, you would perceive your world as a flat circle. You would know there was another side but you would not understand it. If you were suddenly transferred to the other side, you would perceive another dimension. Now you are an astronaut and are launched into space. You look back and there is the whole coin — front, back and edges — suspended in the distance to be seen clearly. This same perception is available to you as you evolve through each experience.

"This situation, as in all situations, was brought into being for a specific reason. It is through the law of opposites that you are being taught, and are teaching yourselves, how to handle energy. Eventually you may become conscious cocreators with the Universal Consciousness. In some ways, the idea of good and evil is helping you to recognize the sacredness of your existence and the responsibility of consciousness. Opposites also provide necessary guidelines for the developing ego.''

CHAPTER ELEVEN

TRUTH

"Explain a little bit about our concept of the truth. What is truth in reality?"

"The doorway to truth is open to every individual but truth is not always revealed in conspicuous forms. Most often it creeps into consciousness through intuition, but it is always recognized when confronted. There is a great fallacy operating throughout the world and that is that there is one great truth — **The Truth** — and when it appears, everyone will know it and be set free. The ocean is truth, so is the sky — a rock is truth, so is a table — an idiot and a genius — an elephant and an insect — all are truth, but there is very little physical similarity.

"Each truth is a new awareness of reality and opens a channel to a variety of new realities. Each individual perceives truth in his or her own way and is in fact a part of the truth perceived. Each truth as it unfolds to the individual in its own way is a new truth. It may not be a new truth to someone else or in terms of the universe, but it is to the individual who embodies it."

"Can you give me an example?"

"Yes, I think I can put it in very simple terms. For instance, when people are confronted by a dark room, they are a bit fearful and apprehensive. But when a light is turned on and the contents of the room revealed, the individuals can see there is nothing to fear. They now walk through the familiar room and are confronted by three doorways to dark and unknown rooms. Now they must go through the same process in order to know the truth about the entire building. That same truth awaits the individual on the street who is yet to enter."

"Must we always be questioning and searching then?" I asked.

"Yes, it is your nature to explore, to learn, to experience and evolve. You see, those who persist in blocking their truths from questions threaten to destroy the validity of their own knowledge. On the other hand, those who are sure of their answers lack the curiosity that could carry them into still greater dimensions of understanding. Any valid expansion of consciousness is part of the greater message. When humanity realizes that they are encountering living truth every day, they will know that truth exists only in those terms. You must understand that you are truth, so discover yourself."

CHAPTER TWELVE
CONSCIOUSNESS

"Would it be correct to assume that the more truth we embody, the more our consciousness expands?"

"Absolutely. Whether you are aware of it or not, your consciousness is expanding to some degree every moment. The consciousness of the individual is in perpetual evolvement, but the rate of evolvement is up to the individual. This is another example of God's promise of freedom."

"Is there any limit to the expansion of our consciousness?"

"No. Even a relatively intense expansion of consciousness barely hints at the possibilities of consciousness that are available to you now. You alway have access to the infinite."

"What can we do to tap this great source of knowledge and truth so we may raise our level of consciousness?"

"First, you must know that the integrity of any intuitive information depends on the inner integrity of the person who receives it. Expansion of consciousness, therefore, requires honest self-appraisal, an awareness of one's own beliefs and prejudices. It brings both a gift and a responsibility. Everyone who wishes to look within themselves in order to find their own answers, to encounter their own appointment with the universe, should therefore become well acquainted with the intimate workings of their own personality.

"Self-knowledge is highly advantageous and in a way its own reward. But it is impossible to look inward with any clarity if you are unwilling to change your attitudes, beliefs or behavior patterns. You must honestly examine those characteristics that are uniquely your own. In other words, you cannot examine reality without examining yourself. You cannot hold encounters with the Universal Consciousness apart from yourself, nor can you separate yourself from your experience.''

"Well, then are we a part of God or are we individuals?''

"Your own physical body is a perfect demonstration of the relationship between you and the Creator. Each cell of your body is an individual but it is also part of the whole you. It cannot be separated from you. It contains within it a memory of everything that is you and can never be changed. It can grow and evolve and improve but it will always be you. The more perfect it is, the more it contributes to the whole.

"The uniqueness that you experience is God's gift to you, but as a living part of God, it is also your gift to God. All that you are and all that you are to become, goes back to the Father and is contained therein. When you realize that God is all and we exist within this great oneness, then you will come to know that our pleasure is God's pleasure and our pain, his pain. The more we learn to express good, the closer we become to our Father. For he created a universe and a world that is in perfect balance and harmony. It is our duty to experience all that has been created with joy and enthusiasm while at the same time being careful not to upset the balance and order established by Law.''

CHAPTER THIRTEEN

WAR

"Is war a part of this balance and harmony or is it an upsetting factor?"

"War is simply another little creation of man's ego. It has become a theater in which a variety of Karmic plays could be enacted. When you realize your oneness with God and your oneness with each other, you will see the fruitlessness of nationalism, racism, and religionism. All are one sharing the Earth as an expression of the one and only God. In this the only enemy is the ego. When it is conquered, humanity's war is over. For the battle is truly within, not without or against others. You must understand that there is no other influence on your existence but your own.

"As your consciousness grows, you will come to realize that the thing you despise most in others is what you despise most in yourself. If you are being criticized, chances are you are very critical yourself. When a problem comes into your life, search within yourself to see where it is coming from. God's way of teaching is by holding a mirror before you. When you see yourself as you really are, you can improve."

"You keep saying that people should search within themselves. How should we do it?"

"In your present frequency of existence, it would be useful to develop a system of meditation. For only by looking quietly within yourself can you experience your own reality. With practice, you can make a connection between your immediate self and the inner identity that is multidimensional. In order to make this connection, there must be a sincere willingness, an acquiescence, a desire. Seek a quiet place, go within and open up channels that will allow you to hear the messages of your intuitive self. Simply relax and listen.

"Every person is surrounded by a thought atmosphere, and this mental atmosphere is a direct result of one's conscious and subconscious thought. This mental atmosphere becomes the direct reason for and cause of everything that comes into a person's life. It is the basis for all the choices an individual makes. It developed before birth and grows through the future. Each person is constantly using this power to attract or repel various choices that he or she is confronted with. Since like attracts like, everyone automatically attracts to themselves just what they are. I know it is difficult to accept, but whatever you are or wherever you are, no matter how intolerable it may seem, you are just where you belong."

"If this is so, then what can we do about it?"

"The only way to change your condition is to recognize that it comes from within you, open a channel of communication with your inner self, and replace the negative or undesirable characteristics with positive or desirable ones. Mankind is fully capable of eradicating misfortune, suffering, want, disease, war and confusion. All humanity has to do is replace these errors with peace, abundance, health, power, life and truth."

"You make it sound so simple. It that really all there is to it?"

He smiled warmly. "It really is that simple but it takes some effort on your part. You see, people who understand the power of prayer and do not use it every day are like the rich man who dies of starvation because he was too frugal to buy food. You have always had the power of prayer at your disposal and you should use it for your own good every single day. By utilizing scientific prayer and meditation as tools for living, you can create whatever vision you have of Heaven right here on Earth and God will bless you for it. You have been limited because you have not known the truth."

CHAPTER FOURTEEN
RELIGION

"What about religion? Where does it fit into all of this?"

"There is nothing new in religion or philosophic invention. If you realize how long humanity has been at this, you would understand the unlikelihood of one's being able to propose a genuinely novel religion or, for that matter, a single verse of religious text that is new."

"But don't you think modern religion is putting people on the right track as far as discovering our true relationship to God?"

"Frankly, today's human beings amaze me. They seem able to go on living year after year, generation after generation without ever pausing to wonder at the sheer miracle of existence itself. They live as though all the world around them were simply a matter of course, a thing to be taken for granted. 'We exist,' they say, 'so what?' Such strange forgetfulness of basic reality, such terrible insensitivity to the miraculous, should well be called a fall from God, or the original sin as your mythological language would have it.

"The world's greatest religions have brought people back time and again to a realization of the ultimate mystery which alone keeps humans afloat, but if they are not aware of this, they have simply missed the whole point of living. An awakening to the miracle of being should be the one and only subject of all religions. But humankind slips from this awareness so easily in order to avoid the responsibility that insight imposes. Therefore people need a spiritual alarm clock to waken them in the midst of their so-called waking lives. Such is the function of religion and its prophets, sages and symbols. It is their mission to focus human awareness on the immense reality of reality.

"Since the task of carrying on always falls into the hands of ordinary people, the original idea gets lost over a period of time. That's when a new alarm clock must ring. Throughout the ages, religions have been victimized by their own tendency to explain themselves in rational terms. Wishing to consolidate their position and power, these religions have appealed to logic and thus cut the ground from beneath themselves. For logic cannot deal with the ineffable, and it is the ineffable that is their inner source of vitality. By being placed in a field of endeavor beyond proof, the miracle of being is beyond doubt. If you believe beyond doubt, it is because you also believe that all being is contained within God, and since anything new that might develop is also within that framework, then the framework is immune to collapse. The miracle of being embraces all that is; but logic embraces only what can be perceived or conceived to exist. It is thus at the mercy of new evidence, which the miracle of being, in embracing all evidence, is not."

"What about faith?"

"Today when you speak of faith or belief, you always mean to imply a certain amount of insecurity. Faith and belief are always accompanied by doubt. Before science became a tyranny as well as a mental discipline, this meaning did not exist. The great heritage of Christianity has become bogged down in modern semantic attitudes and countless fundamentalist doctrines whose conflicting definitions have obscured the nature of both belief and of reason. It is ironic that these fundamentalist sects, which consider themselves to be orthodox, are neither orthodox nor fundamentalist, for fundamentalism is nothing but a recent heresy."

"What do you mean?"

"It is heresy in that the Christian tradition as a whole has seldom until recently known the stubborn insistence on the letter of doctrine that fundamentalists believe essential to Christianity. This did not begin to occur until after the Catholic-Protestant schism of the sixteenth century. It was really the result of a power struggle between controlling factions. The only way to control is to make rules and then convince your followers they are sinning if they break your rules. Most of the rules have little to do with God and reality. In fact, it would be dangerous for these establishments to teach the power of individuality because they would lose their base of control. The more independent the individual, the less chance for control. A truly independent person does not lock the self within the confines of a particular religion, nationality or race because it restricts the opportunity to evolve as a free spirit.

"But there is a fundamentalist revival sweeping the world right now and it seems to be gaining a great deal of support and strength. Many people feel that it is a return to religion and God.

"Yes, this movement is both a blessing and a curse because it is spreading love with one hand while sowing fear, guilt, and hopelessness with the other. The fundamentalist belief in the Devil, suffering, and the end to the world is not only defeatist, but anti-Christian. Christ taught truth and love and hope, not destruction. Because of the power of mass mind, this movement is dangerous. If too many people are brought into this way of thinking, there will be an Armageddon.

"However, there is another revival sweeping across the world and it is a revival of the truth. The world is rapidly moving away from traditions and former ways of life that in a few years will be no more than distant memories. Human life is changing beyond recognition and is passing into an era of unknown experiences. All that humanity will be able to carry with them from the past is the essentials, the things without which they cannot live. I tell you people will be forced to shed the outward trappings of old religions because they will then have to evaluate what is essential in religion and what is merely ornamentation.

"Right now many people think of religion as a church service complete with nostalgic echoes of familiar hymns and prayers. Many would like to preserve the grand cathedral-like structures of doctrine and dogma inherited from the master theologians of medieval Christianity because they fear change. But I say that when your attachment to these things is chiefly nostalgia, they are more a part of your past than of your present or future. You feel nostalgia only for what has been, not for what is. Indeed, so much of the current return to old forms of religion and fundamentalism is nostalgia, prompted by a fear of the unknown, by a terror of being forced out of old familiar beliefs, that you must regard this return with some misgivings.''

''What you have said so far makes a lot of sense but you have to admit that Christianity is a powerful force,'' I said.

''Yes, it is powerful and has lasted primarily because of the underlying truths that established it, not because of church symbology. You must evaluate the truth for yourself. I am simply pointing out that nostalgia is not a true belief in the old faiths but, at most, a recognition that some kind of belief is necessary to you whether you believe in it or not. Thus the hermit crab, having no shell of its own, looks for whatever shell it can find in the interest of its own safety.

''Many people cling to their old beliefs because the concept of change frightens them. They are still afraid of the old Hebrew God of violence and vengeance. They still think the Devil is going to steal their soul and they will fight vehemently to hold on to these limitations. If churches would let go of them for but a moment, their intuition would reveal the truth.

''Since all religions are symbolic, they are all essentially capable of being misunderstood. Today, most religions are sick because there is universal confusion about what is essential and what is not. The essential is a realization of the ultimate behind all being and humanity's relationship to it. This has become confused by semantics and various church doctrines. After all, what proof have you that old religious beliefs are correct? The great majority of people today belong to one religion or another because they inherited it from their parents or the nation of their birth. Although few people can give you a rational reason for why they are Catholic, Baptist, Muslim, Buddhist, Jew or Hindu, they would defend their belonging, not their belief, to the death. Isn't it strange that they would be so vehement in defending something they didn't even choose and may be incorrect?''

''Are you saying that all religions are wrong?''

''No, but the truth behind each religion has been buried beneath a mountain of man-made symbology. You must understand that in the simplest religious terms, you are in God's hands. Whether you like it or not, want it or not, or are aware of it or not, makes no difference. Whether you are an atheist, a skeptic, an agnostic, or an orthodox believer, you are still in the hands of God.

"You may question everything in the world inside and outside of yourself and compare one phenomenon with another, but the being of being has no such comparative identity. It simply is. Therefore the great prophets have been little concerned with the mechanics of religion. However, they have always been concerned, to the exclusion of all else, with God. There is only one power — God. He created the universe and it is perfect. I tell you again that it is humanity's birthright as a creation of God to experience all the goodness, perfection, health and abundance the universe has to offer. If you are not doing this, you are shortchanging yourself. If your religion is not teaching you this, it is shortchanging you.

"There is no doubt that there is mass appeal in the emotional old-time religions, but this appeal is nostalgic and tends to preserve the simplistic beliefs of childhood. The Law requires growth and evolution. Change is inevitable. Innocence retained too long becomes ignorance. **Reality is the goal.**"

CHAPTER FIFTEEN
THE CONFESSION

"Are you saying fundamentalism is ignorance?"

"Absolutely! Today's version of it is perhaps the most blatant form of ignorance in the history of humanity."

"Why are you saying that?" I asked in shock.

"Because millions of well-educated people are not only following, but preaching and defending anti-Christian principles in the very name of Christianity. These enthusiastic evangelists, who espouse the fundamentalist principle of duality, are the false prophets their own prophecy speaks of. They are the representatives of the Antichrist but they don't know it."

"My God, how can you say that?"

"If you do not believe what I am saying, go out and find yourself a born-again Christian and tell him you have not yet received Christ into your heart. Immediately he will commence to pray for you and will sincerely try to save you. However, if you state that you do not believe in Satan or Hell, you will see an altogether different person. He will become defensive and angry and will do everything in his power to prove the existence of evil. He will point out references in the scriptures and will insist that you cannot become a good Christian if you do not believe in the Devil. You cannot believe in just the good, as Christ taught. You must also believe in evil so you can defeat it and be saved. How else can these good people save you if you don't believe in Hell? Some even insist that positive thinking is a demonic form of cultism. This is the greatest of all heresy against the teachings of Christ and yet they do not know it.

"Christ was explicit when he said that no one can serve two masters. Paul in his letter to Corinthians repeated the message when he said, 'Ye cannot drink of the cup of the Lord and the cup of devils; ye cannot be partakers of the Lord's table and of the table of devils.' The First Commandment states specifically that we must believe in one God; and despite all this, fundamentalists insist on a belief in evil and, what is worse, they don't even know why."

The old sage become more and more emphatic as he discussed the fallacy of fundamentalism. He began to shake, and then tears of emotion trickled down his lined cheeks. I could feel the power of his inner conflict and had to choke back a lump in my throat before I could question him further.

"Why are you crying? Do you know why these people believe as they do?"

"Yes, I'm afraid I do. I must confess that it is a result of my doing in another lifetime. I am emotional because after nearly two thousand years I will be able to free myself from the wheel of Karma. I have finally found a way to correct the imbalance I caused during the formative years of Christianity. I am ashamed of the destruction I have caused even though I now understand that it has served a purpose in the whole scheme of things. I have been given a lesson among lessons and now I must be sure every detail of the truth is known so that mankind can be deterred from destroying the world again and can go on to a more advanced level of evolution."

"Can you tell me about it?" I asked sympathetically.

"I was stubborn and rash in those days and it was more important to feed my swollen ego than it was to accept the truth. Even when I recognized the truth, I fought against it just to be disruptive.

"I was born a slave in Persia during the year A.D. 215. My name was Kubrikos. I later adopted the name Manes when I became a spiritual scholar and leader. It was by this name that I became well known to the founders of the Christian ethic. My teachings became a curse to that church and I was the original heretic, the most powerful early rival of Christianity, and they hated me. The bishops did everything in their power to destroy me, my followers and my teachings, but in view of today's Christianity, they failed. When I see a church service or a revival meeting now, I realize I had almost as much impact on Christianity as Christ himself, and yet, few know my name."

"What did you call your teachings? Who were you?"

"As I said, I adopted the name Manes or Mani. My teaching became known as Manichaeism, and although it was totally obliterated, as an organized faith, its ideas went underground and lived on. Many of the ideas tinctured Christian doctrine and persist to this day as a powerful countercurrent to the teachings of Christ. Because of its strength and opposition to Christianity, Manichaeism was considered the supreme heresy. My opponents of the time would be crushed if they heard the fundamentalist preachers of today who begin their sermons by telling their flock that they are all born in sin and must struggle for salvation. You see, it was I who founded the dualistic concept that gave Satan cocreative powers with God, so these people who call themselves Christians are really Manichaeans and do not know it. I am sure they would deny this but it is nonetheless the truth.

"When I was a young slave, I was bought by an older woman who was childless. When she died, she left me a considerable fortune and a heritage of mystical philosophy in the form of metaphysical books. I became quite a scholar and was determined to make my mark on the world. Christianity was a new and growing philosophy and I wanted to contribute my thoughts to the scriptures that were formulating its ethic. However, when the priests became hateful and contemptuous of my ideas, I did all I could to undermine their teachings."

"How could someone outside the church influence what was written in the scriptures?" I asked in fascination.

"I proclaimed myself a comforter, an apostle of Christ. As I said, I inherited a goodly fortune and a set of four books which were originally written by a Saracen called Skythianos, who had been a lover of my mistress. Skythianos was well educated in Arabia at the frontier of Palestine and was a world traveler. In his four books, *Mysteries*, *Chapters*, *Gospel*, and *Treasures*, he taught that the universe is composed of two kingdoms engaged in eternal conflict. One world is light and good, the other darkness and evil. The human spirit is created by God and is therefore good, but the body is created by Satan, a personification of the kingdom of darkness and evil. The light and darkness are completely intermingled inside human beings during life on Earth.

"You see, in this concept, all humanity is ultimately to be purged of darkness and evil by subjugation of the body to the soul. Born of sin, people must get rid of "things of the world" in order to escape the clutches of the Devil and go back to the good Father."

"Well, that certainly sounds familiar, but how did it find its way into Christian doctrine?"

"When I first found out that the prophets and the law recognized only one eternal originator of all things, I decided to travel forth to debate this point with the Christians. However, I had little success in the disputes and decided to resort to magic. In trying to gain an influence in Persia, I offered one of my remedies to an ailing prince, but the prince subsequently died as a result. His father, King Bahman II, had me seized and imprisoned.

"Meanwhile, I had sent three of my disciples to the Christians in Jerusalem in hopes I would fare better if I were known as a Christian. When my men returned, they brought many Christian books and teachings. Utilizing my money, they were also able to get me out of prison. When I made my way to safety in Roman territory, I set about changing the Christian writings to conform with my way of thinking. I mixed my lines into their doctrines wherever they would fit. Later I sent a letter to a Christian by the name of Marcellus who lived at Kaschara in hopes of enlisting his aid in spreading my teachings throughout Rome and Syria.

"Unfortunately, the local bishop, Archelaos, was visiting Marcellus at the time, and Marcellus shared the content of my message with him. The bishop flew into a rage and advised that I be caught and killed on sight as one would kill a wolf or panther. I did not know of this but I became suspicious when my messenger did not return. I was extremely careful when I later visited Marcellus and found out that my host had talked the priest out of his rash ideas. However, Archelaos challenged me to public debate. Four umpires were selected: Marsipus, a pagan scholar, Claudius, a physician, Aegiales, a linguist, and Cleobules, a sophist. These men found in favor of the bishop and against me. The audience became so riled that they tried to stone me, but Marcellus, a true Christian, intervened. Once again I had to take flight.

"Later, when I was safe in Diodoris, I found that the presbyter there was not very skilled in the art of dispute, so I challenged him in hopes of gaining a foothold for my ideas. Unfortunately for me, the presbyter, known as Tryphon, wrote to my old enemy Archelaos and asked how he should deal with me. As things worked out, Archelaos showed up on the day I met the good Tryphon in public debate. Shouting from the audience, the old bishop caused me great humiliation and another defeat. I had to move back to my original haunts in Fort Arabion. Somehow King Bahman II received word of my arrival in Persia and I was seized once again. This time, I was crucified and flayed alive. Then to add further insult, a local taxidermist stuffed my body and put it on display," the old seer related with distaste.

"I guess the Christians weren't very nice in those days," I interjected.

"Let me tell you, back then the worst thing you could call a person was a Manichaean. It was an unmentionable word for it signified a Devil worshiper, an adherent of everything evil or negative. At a time when Christ's teachings were still fresh, a belief in dualism was the greatest heresy. Now it flourishes amongst the hierarchy of the Christian church."

"What ever happened to your books?" I asked.

"The Christian bishops destroyed everything they could get their hands on, including my books on magic and astrology. During those first centuries they did everything they could to stamp out all references to Manichaeism and the Gnostic cults that first espoused the principles of duality from which it sprang. In fact, if it were not for the writings of such church fathers as Tertullian, Iranaeus and Epiphanius of Cypress, nothing would be known of my existence.

"The principal opponent of my teachings became Saint Augustine. He was a Manichaean for nine years but was later converted to Christianity. Once he embodied the truth, he was vehement in his attacks against my doctrines. In the year A.D. 444, Pope Leo had Manichaeism condemned as heretical."

"What else did your doctrines teach besides dualism?"

"I repeat, the basic principle was that there are two unborn self-originating, eternal gods, antagonistic to each other. One was a god of light and good, the other, a god of darkness and evil. The soul of humanity was created by the good god. The body, created by the Devil or darkness, was a part of the realm of matter. Everything on Earth was controlled by the ruler of darkness. This is where the concept that humans were born in sin originated.

"Next I taught that the world was not a creation of God but was made up of creative matter; therefore everything is doomed to perish. This was the origin of the Christian end-of-the-world idea. During another episode of my book on Faith, I had the Father of Greatness create the sky and earth out of the bodies of demons whom Mithra had slain. Thus, whatever people touch, in this world, becomes satanic in matter and basically demonic even though it contains the divine five light elements. This duality included everything, even the human body.

"The Manichaean story of salvation was sort of a distillation process whereby the soul was purified of all matter, first in the moon and then in the sun where they are dissolved and cleansed; the light that was absorbed by darkness is then liberated and ascends back to the Father of Light. The process goes on for a long time until all the light has been reclaimed and humanity is liberated from the Earth. When the good god is heartened by the development of this process, the Devil realizes it will lead to his eventual defeat. Therefore, he comes up with a scheme to put off an end. The Father of Darkness then tells Abraham, the father of man, to go forth and procreate, creating as many people as possible, as numerous as the stars in the sky; for the greater the number of physical beings created, the longer the distillation process will take and, indeed, it will never come to an end. By means of propagation, evil will always be shackled to the world. According to this doctrine, the only way the god of light could win would be for humans to stop reproducing so there is no new evil material to be distilled. This put the curse on sex and formed the church foundation for celibacy.

"In my doctrine of final things to come, I wrote of a world fire that lasts 100 years and brings about the ultimate separation of light from darkness in which the latter will be burned to ashes if humanity cooperates with God strongly enough to bring the fire about. This served as the foundation for the destruction of the world by fire, and it seems modern-day Christians are cooperating psychologically to bring it about. However, the whole idea was erroneous and could prove to be destructive far beyond anything I could have imagined. I cannot believe my original thoughts could have been so powerful or far reaching.

"Today Manichaeism exists nowhere as a confessed or practiced religion or cult, but it has conquered the subconscious of modern people. Christianity only half rejected Manichaeism, destroying it consciously but absorbing much of it subconsciously. It arises from any investigation of the subconscious, psychoanalytical or otherwise; and having been for centuries under repression, it has generated an enormous force. For example, how much of Puritan, rigorous ethic is Christian, based on the doctrines of Jesus Christ, and how much is based on Mani — upon a fear of the body, the instincts, and the natural inclinations of human beings, a belief that essential human nature is not good but evil, a nature that must be destroyed since it cannot be changed.

"Christianity survived because it was literally driven underground where it developed and gathered strength and accumulated to itself an impenetrable mystery. Manichaeism has survived by much the same process, for the unknowable has a stronger grip on our minds than has the knowable. You may well ask yourselves which of the two survives primarily today: are you Christian with a Manichaean subconscious, or Manichaeans with a Christian subconscious? Think about it."

CHAPTER SIXTEEN
CRITICAL MASS

"I can see that these beliefs have caused a considerable amount of psychological damage to humankind but I fail to see how they can lead to world destruction," I commented.

"Apparently I have not made myself clear on the issues of mass mind. You must understand that mass belief, or race consciousness, is a living, breathing form of creative energy which manufactures the basic environmental conditions in which you live. All common belief in health, sickness, government, education, time, and even weather, has a part in it. The only way that a foundation belief can be changed is when a critical number of people are influenced into believing something new. This often happens when the stress of new evidence is placed on society. The world was flat until certain explorers demonstrated that it was round. The Earth was the center of the solar system until astronomers proved that the sun was. People believed that when a light object and a heavy one of the same volume were dropped to the ground, the heavy object would land first. Then Galileo came along and dropped two objects of the same volume from the Tower of Pisa and proved they would strike at the same time.

"Whatever a critical number of people believe becomes part of their experience. If they believe a disease is incurable, it is. If they believe the world will come to an end through atomic annihilation, it will. This is a current and immediate danger."

"I understand what you mean, but how can a belief system be changed?"

"Perhaps it would be of value to tell you a little story about some monkeys," he said with a wry grin.

"Monkeys?"

"Yes, you see, there is a Japanese monkey, *Macaca fuscatta*, which has been observed in the wild for a period of more than 30 years. Beginning in 1952, scientists started dropping sweet potatoes to feed these monkeys which lived on the island of Koshima. The monkeys liked the taste of the raw sweet potatoes but found the dirt on them rather unpleasant.

"Then one day an 18-month-old female named Imo found she could solve the problem by washing the potatoes in a nearby stream. She taught this trick to her mother. Her playmates also learned the new way and taught their mothers, too. Gradually other monkeys picked up the idea, and by 1958 many of the young monkeys were washing the sand from their sweet potatoes.

"Scientists observed that only adults who imitated their children learned this social improvement. Other adults continued to eat dirty sweet potatoes. Then something startling took place. In the autumn of 1958, a certain number of Koshima monkeys were washing sweet potatoes — the exact number is not known. For the sake of example, let us say 99 monkeys on the island had learned to wash their sweet potatoes by that particular morning. Let us further suppose that later that morning, the 100th monkey learned to wash potatoes. Then it happened! By evening almost every monkey in the tribe was washing sweet potatoes before eating them. The added mental energy of this 100th monkey created an ideological breakthrough.

"The scientists were impressed by the sudden acceptance of potato washing on Koshima Island but were astonished when they found that the idea had simultaneously leaped across the sea to other islands and the mainland. Suddenly colonies of monkeys everywhere began washing their sweet potatoes.

"This example demonstrates that when a certain critical number of minds achieves an awareness, this new awareness may be communicated from mind to mind. When only a limited number of people know of a new idea, it may remain the conscious property of the elite. However, there is a point at which if one more person tunes-in to this new awareness, the energy field is strengthened so that the awareness is picked up by almost everyone. This, then, is the basis of your assignment. You must spread your new awareness until critical mass has been achieved."

"How do you expect me to do that? You know there are more than five billion people on the Earth," I objected.

"There are millions who already know the truth and millions more on the threshold of a new awareness growing from within. Many who share the new philosophy are joining together in small groups, and even more are working toward a new truth by themselves without realizing there are others who could help them. The world is in silent revolution. You must join the effort by establishing a network of communications to connect the various groups. Believe me, you will not be alone."

"How will I find these people?"

"Write the book I have given you and they will contact you. The Law states that like attracts like. Small groups are proliferating around the world at this moment. Movements, networks and publications are attracting proponents to the common cause, spreading messages of hope for a positive future. They are citizens of the world transcending political bounds. They have no political structure of their own but they are cooperating with each other for the good of all. They are environmental groups, peace groups, new thought groups, humanists, scientists, and world hunger groups. Their main thrust is a warless society in which people will be free to explore and develop human potential to its fullest. The time has come when human beings can make a quantum leap into the future or take a quantum leap into oblivion. This particular choice belongs to humanity as a whole."

"Will we need to establish a clear majority to reach this critical mass you speak of?"

"History proves that a majority has never been necessary to bring about change. Social reorganization has always been the work of a creative minority. All it takes is a solid effort by a dedicated few. I think Jesus and his disciples demonstrated that point adequately. Because of their size and density, modern societies are subject to great internal fluctuations. You see, they have a limited power of integration. Whenever a disturbance is greater than a society's ability to quell or repress it, the social organization will give way to the new order. In this case, it will trigger a shift to a higher, richer order in which the individual will shine through.''

CHAPTER SEVENTEEN
EVOLUTION

"Revolution begets evolution," the old man stated thoughtfully.

"What do you mean by that?"

"It takes stress or pressure to bring about change. Generally speaking, the underlying cause is the conflict of differing ideas. The most obvious battle line today seems to be between communism and capitalism, or, as each side perceives it, between good and evil. However, the real psychological conflict in society today is between a belief in the end of the world as a result of a battle between good and evil, and a belief in the immortality of the human soul and a world without end.

"When you understand the whole, you understand that there are no such things as good and evil. Differing ideas are a stimulus for creative energy. They also offer each soul an avenue for exploring every aspect of a given concept. In order to defend whichever side of the debate you choose, you must search even the dimmest corner of your consciousness for logical support for your argument. Sometimes this search leads to a crystallization of your position, and at other times it leads to questions and uncertainty. Both are valuable in a search for truth."

"I understand what you are saying, but I can't help but believe that communism is a major threat to humanity and the possible opportunity to explore this individual human potential you have been speaking about," I argued emphatically.

"There is little doubt that the communist doctrine smothers the rights of the individual, but what greater demonstration do you have for the value of individual freedom? When you see an example of life without freedom, you learn to value freedom even more. The competition between the two generates energy. Never fear the outcome. Truth always wins out.

"But I also ask you to consider this: if communism took over the world without threat of competition, would everything then become evil? Are communists a different form of human being? Would Earth life then become a living Hell? On the other hand, if capitalism gained the complete upper hand, would everything be good? Would Heaven reign on Earth? Are all capitalists good? Actually, in the scheme of things, it is the ideological difference which serves humanity best since it serves as a stimulus for achieving. The competition is a source of energy for evolution. This is what must be understood. You are not enemies. You are brothers and sisters helping each other to evolve. It works on the international scale as well as the individual scale."

"Yes, but what happens when someone gets angry enough to kill an enemy?"

"A good question. We have not explored this aspect but we should before I leave. Let me see," he mumbled thoughtfully, "how can I best explain this? Suppose you and a friend are both on a tennis team and are looking forward to playing in a tournament. You agree to play each other every day in order to improve your games. If you kill your friend because he plays different than you, you have not only lost a friend, but a source of energy and an opportunity for further learning. You have not killed his method of playing. Chances are, your tournament opponent will use the same method to defeat you. You have lost on all counts.

"Ideas are living things. They can never be destroyed. You cannot kill an idea, nor can you kill a living soul. They are both immortal and eternal. Killing a human body is simply delaying evolution, both yours and your victim's. Killing is the most ridiculous of mankind's expressions, and mass killing, or war, is the ultimate ignorance. The time has come when humanity must stop using this fruitless exercise as a theater of experience. Only retarded souls would espouse it, and when other retarded souls support it, the result is destruction and the ultimate retardation of eons of human evolution. War is simply a result of one group of ignorant souls trying to exercise control over what God has created. It is the frustrated tantrum of a spoiled child, an ego out of control. Advanced souls should not support these spoiled children.

"The question at hand today is, do you create Armageddon and go back to primeval beginnings, or do you defeat ignorance and create a new world in which the individual, working in cooperation with other individuals and utilizing universal powers, rules supreme. A world in which there is no need to lead or to follow. A world where people take responsibility for themselves and take charge of their own evolution without blaming others for their shortcomings.

"Remember, God created us all in his own likeness. God is an open-ended, eternal dissipative system; the universe is an open-ended, eternal dissipative system; the world is an open-ended, eternal dissipative system; humanity is an open-ended eternal dissipative system, and so is every cell in the human body. They are all in eternal evolvement. It is a highly organized, flowing wholeness which is always in the process of becoming. The system is maintained by a continuous consumption of energy which is provided from within. Each system, like a seed, contains the energy necessary to reach its full potential. If God were a seed, we would be a seed within a seed within a seed, etc. When the seed reaches its full potential, it provides energy back to the original creative source.

"Creativity is a result of the continuous movement of energy through the system. This energy flow causes fluctuations in individual systems and if the fluctuations are large enough, they perturb the system and alter its structural integrity. In other words, they shake up the old pattern and cause the parts to come together in new ways. A new whole is reorganized from the old parts and it is generally of a higher order. Universal Law demands that each reorganization results in a higher form of complexity. This is evolution. It is just as true as the law of gravity and much more powerful. It is true in the universe, in people and in society. There is no difference."

"You know you have given me a great deal to digest and many of your ideas are very controversial. Will everyone understand all of this or will I just be starting another international argument?"

"You must not argue. Your duty is to communicate. No argument or discussion can bring truth to those who are not ready to receive it. A good teacher knows that most of teaching is but the planting of seeds. For every idea a student understands, there will be a hundred that will come into conscious recognition only after the mind is ready to understand and accept them. However, you must not be concerned, for there are many who are ready to receive these truths and join their energy with yours. It is time for a reorganization of the old parts."

CHAPTER EIGHTEEN
REVELATIONS

A gentle breeze brought a slight chill to the air, and growing shadows in the valley below reminded me that I should be heading down the mountain soon. I knew I should leave but I couldn't seem to break the spell this mystical old man held over me. I wanted to hear more. I wanted to absorb all the wisdom I could from him. By now I was relatively sure I was talking to a messenger of God and yet a nagging doubt kept marching through the pit of my stomach. Everything the man said made exceptional sense and demonstrated a knowledge far beyond ordinary human perception, but I still seemed to need some kind of tangible proof. I don't know exactly what I expected him to do and I was a bit annoyed at my own skepticism.

"I must go soon," he said, "but since humankind always seems to need prophecies, I will give you my version of revelations. A new era has begun and a far more sane and just world will evolve. During the next century mankind will go through a complete spiritual metamorphosis. Inner abilities will be revealed to the world and humans will be set free from many of the restraints that have bound you in the past. Because of this new self-understanding, mankind's militant nature will soften and individuals will become much more aware of their true relationship to the planet Earth, the universe, and their freedom within what they understand as time.

"When humanity's ego is freed from false fears, it will open the conscious mind to many truths that had previously been blocked out. Once this channel is open, human consciousness will expand dramatically and new powers will become available. Areas of the physical brain that had been inactive will be put to use. Mankind will then become much more sensitive and perceptive. When this new sensitivity comes into play, a vast array of new colors, sights, sounds and smells will be revealed. This will bring a whole new spectrum of beauty into human experience and a whole new sensual base. To this point, you have only had need of about five percent of the computer you call brain, but now you will find need to tap more of its latent potential.

"It is difficult to give an explanation of these things in your terms since your concept of yourself is so limited and restricted. You are so much more than what you perceive, that it is impossible for you to imagine. The power, energy, creativity and intelligence being utilized by you is like a grain of sand compared to the mass of the Earth. The time has come to raise your conscious awareness of the power that is within you as an individual soul and to instruct you in the use of energy for broader, more enriching experiences on the Earth plane. Believe me when I say that you have not yet scratched the surface.

"When humankind realizes that all needs can be provided by mind, without struggle or without taking from other humans, a new spirit of cooperation will arise. The strong attitude of competition will dissolve and with it, the fears, mistrust and anxieties that cause wars, disharmony and disease. Humanity will no longer feel the necessity of defending national, political or religious boundaries; for in recognizing the power of one's own individuality, people will also assume responsibility for themselves. Men and women won't need to be led nor will they feel the necessity of leading.

"This does not mean life will turn into Utopian dullness, for there will always be challenges. These challenges will be perceived in a new way and from a different power base. In time, humanity will become more aware of the expansion of personal individual evolution. As each person on Earth becomes more aware of the individual soul, he or she will be able to open channels of receptivity which will provide access to greater sources of power, energy and knowledge.

"Intuition will grow stronger as the ego drops its defense against psychological and psychic communications between the Earth self and the universal self. Mankind is indeed on the threshold of a new era. An era of awareness, an era of growth and an era of freedom and individuality. As you come to know, you will know that you know and you will rejoice in the great awareness that is the Universal Mind.

"Human beings will experience a different kind of existence. When all people realize their oneness with each other and recognize that they have played all the roles, no one will look down on an individual from another race, no sex will be considered better than another, nor will any role in society be judged better than another. Each individual will become aware of his or her own experience at many levels of society and in many roles. This new open consciousness will then feel its connection with all other living beings, and the continuity of consciousness will have to change since they all have been based on current beliefs.

"Future children will learn from birth that their basic identity is not dependent upon their body. They will also learn that time, as it has been known, is really an illusion. Children of the future will be consciously aware of many of their past experiences and they will learn to identify with the old man or woman they will become in the future. This means that many of the lessons that come with age will be available to the young. However, the old will not lose the spiritual elasticity of their youth. For practical reasons, future incarnations will still remain hidden from the entity. But when new areas of the physical brain become activated, it will become possible to get brain readings that will reveal past-life memories.

"Now, you must understand that all of these alterations are spiritual changes in which the meaning of religion will escape organized bounds, become a living part of individual existence, and where psychic frameworks rather than physical ones will form the foundations for civilization. Religion as it is known today will cease to exist, but prayer and meditation will become part of the daily routine.

"Humanity's experience will become so extended that humans will seem to have changed into another being. This does not mean there will be no problems, but it does mean that people will have far greater resources at their disposal to solve them with. It also presupposes a richer and far more diverse social framework where men and women will find themselves relating to each other not only as people they are, but as people they were. Some of the greatest changes will be in family relationships. There will eventually be room for emotional interactions within the family that are now impossible. The conscious mind will be more aware of subconscious material and will have to evaluate at that level.

"Since reincarnation is inherent in the deeper truths, it will be automatically recognized and accepted by the entire human race. As humanity attains that plateau of deeper perception, you will come to understand that the aura is the weather vane of the soul. It can show which way the winds of destiny are blowing. Every person radiates an aura of colors about their head and shoulders which indicates their true emotional state. The various colors represent sickness, dejection, love, fulfillment and joy. This will be the next evolutionary step for humankind. Everyone will be able to see and read auras.

"You will learn that an aura is an effect, not a cause. Every atom, every molecule, every group of atoms and molecules, however simple or complex, tells a story of itself, its purpose and its pattern through the vibrations that emanate from it. As the soul of an individual travels through the realm of being, it shifts and changes its pattern as it uses or abuses the opportunities presented to it. The human eye perceives these vibrations as colors. Thus at any time, in any world, a soul will radiate its history through its vibrations. When another soul apprehends these vibrations and understands them, it will know the state of its fellow soul and the progress made. At this point in evolution, people will have to be totally honest for there will no longer be such a thing as deceit. If a soul planned to lie, it would show in the aura.

"Danger, catastrophe, accidents, death, will not come unannounced. You will see them on their way as did the prophets of old. You will be projected into a world where people see each other's faults and virtues, their weaknesses and strengths, their sickness, their misfortunes and their coming success. You will see yourselves as others see you and will be an entirely different race of people. If you must believe in a salvation, then this is it. Just ask yourself how many of your vices would persist if all them were known to everyone?

"The latent power of mental concentration is also due to increase along with mental telepathy. Even now at times you are able to sense what others are thinking and even when you don't recognize it, you know the trend their thoughts are taking. Always remember that God speaks to all of Its parts through the living soul-stuff of each consciousness. The messages are subtle. When the time comes for knowing, that which is needed is revealed. There is but one mind.

"I have explained that the spirit of humanity is on a journey of enlightenment through perpetual evolution. Now a new light is shining on the world and it will illuminate a kaleidoscope of new experiences for mankind. The time has come to realize that the veil between spirit and matter is very thin. You must learn that the invisible passes into visibility through your faith in it. A new science, a new religion and a new philosophy are rapidly unfolding in the hearts and minds of people and you must understand that this is in line with the evolution of the Great Presence and nothing can hinder its progress.

"There are those who would try to harness this new knowledge for their own gain as the religions of old did. I hereby warn these individuals that it will be useless as well as foolish to make any attempts to cover this principle or to hold it as a vested right of any religious sect or order. The truth will spring forth throughout the world and the spirit will make itself known.

"Many in their ignorance will struggle against the change, wanting desperately to cling to the old ways, but after much weeping and gnashing of teeth, the transition will be made and the Earth experience will become a far more pleasant experience in humanity's journey to enlightenment.

"Now! I have given all that I have come to give and I can no longer remain focused in this plane of existence. My energy field is almost exhausted. You will have to carry on the work from this point forward. Work with faith and know that you are not alone. There is no one savior; many have been given the message.''

The old Indian began to fade right before my eyes. First he became transparent, then he seemed to break into millions of electronic particles which ultimately condensed into a concentrated ball of mysterious light. The light remained suspended for a moment, then flew off into the heavens.

I stood on the promontory, cold, lonesome and confused. I knew the direction of my destiny but I did not know how to begin the journey. It was an honor to be chosen but I wasn't sure I wanted to become so involved in the human condition. I was a loner because I hated responsibility, and now I would have to crawl out of my shell to take on the ultimate responsibility. I didn't know whether I wanted to but then again I wasn't sure I had a choice. I retreated from the mountain in a trance and decided to let my intuition guide me one day at a time. This book is my first effort.

Afterword: The Metaphysical Sower

Who Hath Ears to Hear, Let Him Hear:

God is the sower, his seed is the truth.
He distributes it equally to the wise and uncouth.
Universal Wisdom is the truth of life,
It is available to you if you'll give up your strife.

The seeds of reality fall on all types of soil,
The magic they carry can relieve your toil.
They fall by the wayside, in rocks and in ditches,
But where the soil is fertile, these seeds bear riches.

If your mind is a wayside, a briar patch or gravel,
Go to the mountain and ask to unravel
The mystery that can cultivate your mind,
Into the fertile garden where you will find

The fruits of God's love: peace, health and prosperity,
More than enough wisdom to last through posterity.

Each of our minds represents qualities of soil
So we are responsible if seeds flourish or spoil.
With paternal love God created us free.
He gave us ears to hear and eyes to see.

But we must be willing to perceive that deeper meaning
Than the physical wonders our senses are gleaning.
We must open our eyes to the greater reality
That mankind is spirit without partiality.

There is one great mind of which we are a part,
But what you see of this world, is what you bear in your heart.
The world you create is your path to the truth,
Nothing can hurt you if you keep aloof.

If along the way, you forget who you are,
Negatives will enter and lead you afar.
There are lessons to be learned in this land of five senses,
But we must learn to interpret them in spiritual tenses.

So cultivate your garden and prepare your soil
To receive the seeds of wisdom which relieve your toil.
Give thanks to the sower for the glory of life,
Put down your shovel and give up your strife.

Celebrate this world and watch your seeds flourish
Into goodness and love that will eventually nourish
The eternal consciousness that we all cherish.

Behold! A New Awareness Is at Hand!

INNER VISIONS SERIES

The Inner Visions Series explores inner realities and individual evolution. Some titles are biographical, while others describe methods of spiritual awakening. The purpose is to share with many the experiences of those whose vision of life reaches beyond limited realities to encompass a larger view of the universe.

Spirit Guides: We Are Not Alone
by Iris Belhayes
The message of this book is that we are **not** alone, that we are surrounded at all times by love and support. The aim of this book is to help readers find their way back "Home" to the love which is there whenever we choose to experience it.
ISBN 0-917086-80-5 $12.95

The Mystery of Personal Identity
by Michael Mayer
Psychology meets astrology in this exploration of that ancient question: "Who am I and what does my life mean?" The author leads readers on a journey beginning with his own forty night vision quest in the woods alone, to Native American and other ancient and modern traditions of personality theory.
ISBN 0-917086-54-6 $9.95

Past Lives Future Growth
by Armand Marcotte and Ann Druffel
This book tells the amazing story of the psychic counseling of Armand Marcotte. His three guides "feed" him information when he is fully conscious. They and Armand had been monks together in an earthly life in a monastery in Europe. Armand had fallen behind in his spiritual development. His former friends are helping him to help others so he can "catch up" and, someday, rejoin them.
ISBN 0-917086-88-0 $12.95

Hands That Heal
by Echo Bodine Burns
This unique book is written by a spiritual healer eager to share her gift with other people. Convinced that **anyone** can channel healing energy, the author offers her insights and understanding of the healing process.
ISBN 0-917086-76-7 $7.95

The Psychic and the Detective
by Ann Druffel with Armand Marcotte
A murder most foul has been committed. **The police are baffled**. All clues lead to dead ends. In many cities, the young, beautiful victim would become another statistic in the files of unsolved crimes. *The Psychic and the Detective* offers not only a "good read" in terms of excitement and drama, but also hope and inspiration that the American dream of "justice for all" may yet be achieved.
ISBN 0-917086-53-8 $7.95

A New Awareness
by Jack Nast
The world is on the threshold of a major evolutionary shift which will catapult us from an era of fear and superstition into a consciousness of individual power and psychic knowing. Through a wise old Indian, Jack Nast channels images of the coming changes. Topics such as God, religion, war, reincarnation, karma, thought, soul, ego, reality, truth and much more are discussed with wisdom and elegance.
ISBN 0-917086-94-5 $9.95

Order from:

ACS PUBLICATIONS, INC., DEPT. AWV987 • PO BOX 16430 • SAN DIEGO, CA 92116-0430
FOR PEOPLE WHO LOOK AHEAD